Food Chains

Written by Sally Mo

D1610495

Contents

Collins

Essential food

All living things need food to survive. Food gives them energy to move around and grow. **Organisms** get their food from their **environment**.

Living together

The plants and animals that live together in a particular place, such as a forest or a rock pool, form a **community**. They depend on each other to survive. Some of the organisms make food, while others eat it. The links between a food **producer** and a food **consumer** form a food chain.

Who eats who?

A food chain shows who eats who in a community. For example, grass is eaten by rabbits, which are eaten by foxes. There are many different examples of food chains in a community.

Producers are the start of a food chain. These are the organisms that can make their own food so they don't need to eat! Most food producers are plants.

The producers are eaten by the consumers, which are the organisms that can't make food. Instead, consumers eat ready-made food. They do this by eating plants and other animals. People are consumers, and so are cats, dogs, cows and sheep.

grass

fox

rabbit

5

Capturing the sun

Plants are essential. Without plants, animals couldn't survive.

Green leaves

Plants make their own food using sunlight. They hold out their green leaves so they can trap as much sunlight as possible. They make sugars and a gas called oxygen. Oxygen is invisible and it's found in air. We need oxygen to breathe.

Leaves have a large surface to trap sunlight.

Sugars and starches

The sugars are moved around and used by the plants to grow, but sometimes they are stored for future use. Plants change the sugars into starch, which can be stored in their roots.

Root vegetables such as parsnips contain starch.

All sorts of producers

There are many different types of plants. Some are tiny, but others are huge, like trees.

Living in water

Algae are plants that live in water. They are important because many of the animals that live in water feed on them. This includes the world's largest fish, the whale shark. Seaweeds are algae too. They grow in shallow water where there's a lot of light. Some seaweeds are green, but others are red or brown, and the largest grow up to 80 metres long!

The largest seaweed is the giant kelp which can grow to 80 metres in length.

The leaves of the trees form a roof over the forest.

Giant producers

The largest plants are trees. Trees are found in places such as forests where they grow close together. Their leaves, flowers and fruits are eaten by a great many animals.

Essential grass

Grass is an important plant. It's eaten by **grazing** animals, such as cows and sheep.

Long leaves

A grass plant has long leaves and deep roots. Its leaves grow from the bottom. This means they can be nibbled by animals and grow back. That's why lawns have to be cut every week in summer!

Cereal foods

One group of grasses are called **cereals**. Wheat, barley, maize, oats and rice are all cereals. Cereal plants produce lots of large seeds, which we harvest to eat and to feed to our farm animals.

Wheat seeds are harvested and ground up to make flour.

Cows wrap their long tongues around grass leaves and pull them into their mouths.

The African savannah

The savannah is the name given to the vast, flat lands covered in grasses and found in Southern Africa.
The savannah is home to many millions of grazing animals.

Herds of grazing animals eat the grasses.

The leaves of the acacia tree are eaten by **browsing** animals, such as giraffes.

The savannah is covered in grasses.

Vultures pick over dead remains or circle in the sky looking for food.

The grazing animals are preyed upon by **predators**, such as lions. The lions get a good view of the herds from this rocky hill.

The dung (poo) of grazing animals is food for this dung beetle.

13

Plant eaters

There are many different types of plant eaters.
They include antelopes, parrots, zebras, locusts, slugs
and snails. These animals are often called **herbivores**.

Most plant eaters eat leaves, but other parts of a plant
can be eaten too, such as the stems, flowers, fruits, seeds
and even the roots and bark. Some animals eat the whole
plant, but others are fussy and only eat bits of a plant.
Some only eat certain types of plants. For example,
the giant panda eats only bamboo, while the koala likes
eucalyptus leaves.

Finches have short but strong beaks that are perfect for cracking open seeds.

Hummingbirds sip the sugary nectar found in flowers.

Locusts are insects with strong jaws for chewing leaves.

15

Chewing leaves

Some leaves are soft and easy to eat, just like salad leaves.
But sometimes leaves are tough and difficult to eat.
Animals have special ways of eating these tough leaves.

Flat teeth

Grazing animals, like sheep and horses, have large, flat
teeth, which they use to grind leaves. This breaks up
the leaves and forms a mush which they swallow.

Cows and sheep have an extra-large stomach too.
Once their food has been churned around in the stomach,
it comes back to the mouth for a second chew. This is
called chewing the cud. These animals spend hours
chewing their food, even when they're resting.

Rabbits produce two types of poo – soft poo and
hard poo. Rabbits eat the soft
poo so that it passes through
their gut again and they
can get more **nutrients**
from their food.

A sheep can move its jaw side
to side to grind the grass.

The elephant uses its long trunk to reach leaves on branches high up in the tree.

17

Flowers, fruits and nuts

Many animals like to eat fruits and nuts. Flowers are tasty too. This is because many flowers produce a sugary liquid called nectar that animals love.

Monkeys love to eat sweet-tasting fruits.

Sweet nectar

Bees and other insects visit flowers to drink the nectar and collect pollen. Pollen is the yellow dust found inside flowers. Many other animals visit flowers for their nectar too, including bats and hummingbirds.

Tough nuts

Nuts have a tough outer case that has to be cracked to reach the seed inside. We use nutcrackers to open nuts. Toucans and macaws use their strong beaks like nutcrackers. The agouti, a rat-like animal from South America, is one of the few animals that can eat Brazil nuts by gnawing a hole in the case.

The meat eaters

Plant eaters aren't the only animals in a food chain. The plant eaters are eaten by other animals known as meat-eating animals or carnivores.

Predator and prey

A meat eater is a predator because it hunts other animals. The animals that it hunts are called prey. For example, a cheetah is a predator and it hunts prey animals, such as antelope and gazelle.

Cheetahs are predators that rely on speed to catch their prey.

There are always fewer predators than prey animals in one area. If there were more predators, they'd eat all the prey animals and run out of food.

Some animals have a mixed diet of meat and plant foods and are called omnivores, like chimpanzees and wild boars. People are omnivores too.

Catching their prey

Predators have to be able to find, catch and then kill their prey. They do this in many ways.

Senses

Predators use their senses to find their prey. Frogs have good eyesight and they can spot the slightest movement made by their prey. Sharks have an amazing sense of smell to find their prey in the water. Owls use their hearing to catch prey animals in the dark.

When a chameleon spots an insect, it shoots out its long, sticky tongue to catch it.

Catching prey

Eagles swoop down and grip their prey using their hooked claws and powerful beak. Brown bears use their sharp claws to grip slippery fish. Wasps and scorpions sting their prey to kill them.

Spiders catch flying insects by spinning a web of sticky threads.

A rainforest food chain

A rainforest is a special type of forest found near the equator where it's warm and wet all year round.

The trees form a roof over the forest. Their leaves are eaten by many different types of animals including insects, monkeys and sloths.

The slowest moving animal of the rainforest is the sloth. It has long arms which end in huge hooked claws. It spends the day hanging from branches. It eats leaves, fruits and young twigs.

The harpy eagle is one of the world's largest eagles. It flies from tree to tree looking for food. Its favourite foods are sloths and monkeys.

The forest floor is covered with fallen leaves, twigs, fruits and nuts, as well as the remains of dead animals. Everything is broken down by fungi and small animals, like beetles.

The top consumer

The top consumers are the animals at the end of the food chain. These are the animals that aren't hunted by other animals. They have no natural enemies.

Only a few

There are always fewer meat eaters than plant eaters. The last animal in the chain, the top consumer, is fewest in number. Top consumers are often large animals, such as eagles, lions, tigers, wolves and great white sharks. They eat a lot of food so there'll only be a few of them in a large area. For example, there may only be one family of tigers living in a forest the size of a town.

The bald eagle is a hunter; it isn't hunted by other animals.

A pack of wolves hunts over a very large area.

A desert food chain

Deserts are dry places where it hardly ever rains. Some deserts are hot too. Few plants can survive in deserts and this means there are very few animals.

The prickly pear is a type of cactus. It has thick leaves covered in spines. Its fruits are eaten by many animals.

The short-horned grasshopper eats the flowers of the prickly pear cactus.

The rattlesnake spends the day coiled up under shrubs and rocks, or in burrows. It emerges at night to hunt lizards and small mammals. The rattlesnake shakes the tip of its tail to make a rattling noise to warn other animals to stay away.

The collared lizard hunts grasshoppers, catching them in its powerful jaws. When it runs fast, it lifts its front legs and runs on its hind legs.

Scavengers

Scavengers are animals that don't hunt other animals. They feed on animals and plants that are already dead. They help to clean up their environment.

Food fights

A dead animal on the savannah quickly attracts scavengers, such as vultures, hyenas and jackals. Vultures can spot a dead body from the air and are often first to reach the food. Hyenas and jackals follow. They gather around and pick over the meat left on the bones. Hyenas and jackals prey on animals too, but it's easier to finish off the food left by other hunters! Sometimes, they steal the food from lions.

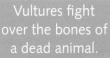
Vultures fight over the bones of a dead animal.

The hyena has
a powerful jaw that can
crack open large bones.

31

Waste disposal

Nothing goes to waste in nature. An army of small animals eats all the rotting remains on the ground. Without them, wild places would be littered with rotting bodies, piles of poo and layers of fallen leaves.

Dealing with waste

Flies lay their eggs in dead bodies. Within a few days, a huge number of maggots hatch and eat the rotting food. Earthworms pull dead leaves into their burrows in the soil and eat them. Slugs, snails, woodlice and many others living on the ground help to break down this waste too.

The earthworm feeds on dead leaves on the ground.

Woodlice feed on rotting wood.

Fallen apples are eaten by many small animals as well as fungi.

Recycling

The smallest organisms feeding on the dead and decaying remains are the bacteria and fungi. They're called **decomposers**. Their job is vital, as they help to recycle valuable nutrients.

Fungi

Fungi live in the ground. Some are tiny and invisible to the eye. Others are formed of long threads that grow through the soil. In autumn, you see many fungi when they appear above ground as toadstools.

In autumn, toadstools appear on woodland floors.

Back to plants

As the dead matter is broken
down, nutrients are released
into the soil. These are taken
up by plant roots. This means
that the nutrients that were
in plants, and then eaten by
animals, end up back in the soil.
They've been recycled.

An ocean food chain

The oceans are home to many different types of plant and animal. Most live in the top layer of the oceans where there's plenty of light.

The tiny plants floating in the ocean are called plankton. They use sunlight to make food.

Krill are animals that look like small prawns. They are found in huge shoals (groups) and they feed on plankton.

The salmon are hunted too, by larger predators in the ocean such as killer whales. Killer whales live in groups called pods and they hunt together.

The salmon is a predator. It's a large, fast-swimming fish with a powerful body. It chases and catches small fish.

Small fish like to eat krill.

A food web

A food chain shows how one animal or plant is eaten
by another. In the wild, one animal may eat lots of
different plants and be preyed upon by different animals.
For example, birds such as the thrush may eat caterpillars,
snails, worms and even berries.

Linked together

If you drew all the food chains in one community on
a piece of paper, you'd get lots of lines criss-crossing from
one animal to another. This creates a food web.

Song thrushes love to eat snails, but they'll eat other foods too.

A food web is made up of many food chains with lots of links.

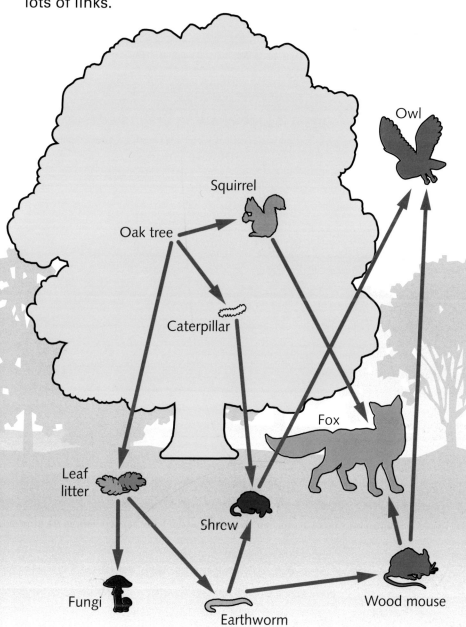

Out of balance

Food chains are easily upset. A change in the number of one animal can affect the survival of all the others in the food chain.

Many things can upset a food chain. A fire may destroy the trees, a disease may kill some of the animals or people may hunt them.

A forest fire can wipe a whole community.

If there are too many zebras, they'll eat all the grass.

Imagine there's an increase in the number of zebras on the savannah. Then there's more food for lions and they increase in number too. But the extra zebras eat too much grass. Eventually, all the grass is eaten, which means the zebras can't find enough food and so they move away or die. Then the lions also run out of food and they die too.

Protecting the animals

Sometimes the changes that upset food chains are caused by people. For example, some people pay a lot of money to hunt top consumers such as lions and leopards. Taking too many fish from the oceans or destroying rainforest trees breaks food chains too.

Controlling the amount of fish that can be caught makes sure there's enough food for other animals in the oceans.

Saving animals

There are many organisations that work to protect animals. But to successfully protect an animal, they have to look after all the different plants and animals in a food chain. You can't protect just one animal: you have to make sure that the plants it eats or the animals it hunts are saved too.

National Parks are places where the whole environment is protected, and people can enjoy watching wildlife

Glossary

browsing   eating leaves

cereals   grass-like plants with large seeds which we harvest and eat

community   a group of plants and animals that live in the same place

consumer   an animal that has to find food to eat; some eat just plants, others eat only other animals and some have a mixed diet

decomposers   living things such as bacteria and fungi that break down dead and decaying matter

environment   an organism's surroundings

grazing   eating grasses

herbivores   animals that eat plants

nutrients   substances in food needed for healthy growth

organisms   living things, such as animals or plants

predators   animals that kill other animals for food

producer   a living thing, such as a plant, that can make its own food

scavengers   consumers that eat dead and decaying matter

Index

Links in a food chain

Plant eaters
These animals
are often
called herbivores.

Producers
living things, such
as plants, that
can make their
own food

Decomposers
living things such as
bacteria and fungi that
break down dead and
decaying matter

Predators
animals that kill
other animals
for food

Top predators
animals that eat
other animals but
no other animals
feed on them

Ideas for reading

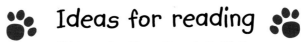

Written by Clare Dowdall, PhD
Lecturer and Primary Literacy Consultant

Reading objectives:
- retrieve and record information from non-fiction
- discuss their understanding and explain the meaning of words in context
- identify main ideas drawn from more than one paragraph and summarise ideas

Spoken language objectives:
- give well-structured descriptions, explanations and narratives for different purposes

Curriculum links: Science: animals – food chains; Geography – locational knowledge

Resources: ICT, pens and paper, world map

Build a context for reading

- Ask children to explain what they think a food chain is. Introduce the term "predator", and ask for ideas about its meaning.
- Look at the front cover. Ask children to describe what is happening, and to suggest a food chain that includes an osprey and a fish.
- Read the blurb together. Ask children to think about what they like to eat and how this is the beginning of a food chain.

Understand and apply reading strategies

- Turn to the contents. Discuss how the information in this book is organised and presented, and what kind of book this is (a report and an explanation).